CW00401156

MOBILE
MADNESS

First published in Australia in 1997 by New Holland Publishers Pty Ltd
Sydney•London•Cape Town•Singapore

Produced and published in Australia by
New Holland Publishers Pty Ltd

3/2 Aquatic Drive	24 Nutford Place	80 McKenzie Street
Frenchs Forest	London W1H 6DQ	Cape Town 8001
NSW 2086 Australia	United Kingdom	South Africa

Cartoons by Mark Lynch
Printed in Australia by Australian Print Group

Publishing General Manager: Jane Hazell
Publishing Manager: Averill Chase
Designer: Patricia McCallum
Editor: Jacquie Brown

ISBN 1 86436 316 9

Special thanks to Cyndi Kaplan who encouraged our concept from its inception
and whose book, *Publish for Profit,* demystified the process, and gave us the know-how
and courage to take it to the marketplace.

MOBILE MADNESS

A Guide to Mobile Phone Etiquette

Latife Hayson ◆ Lisa Tiver ◆ Mark Lynch

NEW
HOLLAND

This is a helpful guide on how to spot a mobile phoney and how to avoid becoming one yourself.

It's inspired by and dedicated to all the 'Swinging Dicks' and 'Jockettes,' whose ring tones have interrupted everything from spine-tingling arias to lustful, unbridled moments of passion.

Once upon a time you could only judge your date by getting access to their house, fridge, books and CD collection. Now you needn't enter the home to get the real picture, you can do it in the first five minutes by observing their mobile phone behaviour.

Constantly stroking, caressing or playing with your mobile in public
– the only person it's turning on is you.

Carrying your mobile in your trouser pocket – false advertising!

Choosing your mobile for its size, weight and colour (the only time men brag about having the smallest!).

Talking on your mobile with your digit finger firmly planted in the other ear.

Displaying your mobile on a bar, throwing it onto a restaurant table or wearing it on your belt – confirmation of insecurity.

Hideous and intrusive ring tones.

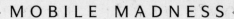

Faking a deal on your mobile and it rings.

Giving your lover a mobile so you know where she is at all times, *and* paying the bill so you know exactly who she rings.

Raising your handbag to your ear at the ring of a mobile.

Taking a call during sex.

Seeing a stranded driver and not offering to call for assistance.

Instructing your hairdresser to stop the blow job while you answer your mobile phone.

Knocking on your date's door while on the mobile – finish your conversation first, they're not that desperate to see you.

Spending your entire date on the mobile.

Arriving at an expensive restaurant while on your mobile, tossing the keys to the valet parking attendant, then entering the restaurant still talking on the mobile.

Having two mobiles.

Trying to talk on two mobiles at once.

Taking a mobile phone to the beach with your share portfolio
(and it's Saturday).

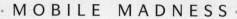

Being photographed for the business section of a daily paper while talking on your mobile phone.

Answering your mobile phone and announcing,
'I can't talk, I'm in a meeting.'

Competing with other mobile dependants in the world's largest public phone box, the Qantas Club. Even less cool is to be on your mobile at the gate. At least you're not alone in the Qantas Club ...

Silly voicemail messages.

Using your mobile to make an internal office call.

Ignoring announcements and signage to switch off all mobile phones.

Cancelling a date on your mobile, with party noise in the background.

Giving a mobile as a gift, then using it as a tracking device.

Answering your mobile while in the shower with a lover.

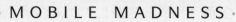

Answering your mobile while exposing yourself at the urinal.

Juggling your gearstick and mobile in your convertible:
'I'm important, rich and in demand!'

Using your mobile on a ski lift, motor scooter, tennis court
or while roller-blading.

Your mobile phone ringing in an art gallery, the theatre,
opera or the movies.

Displaying your mobile phone on the bar when it's switched off.

Using the excuse 'Gotta go, my battery's about to run out' to extract yourself from a conversation you don't want to have.

Answering your mobile in your office while on two other calls and speaking to your secretary at the same time.

Talking to one client on your mobile while in a meeting with another. Who is paying for this time?

Taking a call at your lover's when it's your spouse: 'Darling, I'll be there in a minute.'

Ringing your mates after sex.

Being invited to dinner at your best friend's place and taking social calls through the pre-dinner drinks, entree, main course, dessert and coffee.

Being caught having an affair from your mobile phone bills.

His and hers matching mobiles.

Buying your child a mobile to match yours.

Waiting for a crowd before you make your call.

Flashing it in public.

Calling your date on approach to make sure they're outside and waiting and worse still, pulling up outside and honking your horn since you are too busy to knock. After all, you are on an important call.

Taking your mobile to the beach and turning it off so you won't be disturbed.

Depositing your latest flame in one aisle of the supermarket and dashing to another to call the ex to get the recipe for your favourite dish.

Standing in a long queue and calling a contact inside to come and save you.

Coaching your wife through childbirth via the mobile.

Taking a call from your partner while away on a business trip, then hanging up and saying, 'That was just a friend.'

Constantly taking mobile calls while being briefed by a new client.

While chatting someone up, answering your mobile and it's your other half on the line.

Competing to see who uses the most batteries during one lunch: CBD yuppies' lunchtime sport.

Debating in public about who has the best value-added features and services for their mobiles.

Explaining that it's your mobile, not your vibrator, when it goes off in a meeting.

Being turned on by the sound of your own authoritative voice
whenever you're on your mobile.

Putting your mobile number on your answering machine and then
diverting your mobile back to your answering machine.

Secretly swapping SIM cards at a dinner party and changing
the victim's message.

Watching your mobile, hoping it will ring.

Taking your mobile to bed, hoping he might remember to call.

Disturbing the peace to arrange your social life.

Phoning the waiter from the restaurant table to place your order.

Having to reschedule a meeting because all attendees have spent the entire meeting talking on their mobiles.

Sharing your social life with the whole restaurant.

Driving while using your mobile earpiece and crashing head-on into a speeding ambulance.

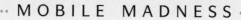

Seating yourself at a restaurant table and announcing to the table *and* the restaurant, 'Sorry, I can't turn the mobile off, I'm waiting for an overseas call.'

Sending make-up, tissues and tampons flying as you feverishly search through your handbag for your ringing mobile.

Dating and operating a mobile simultaneously.

Teaming your mobile with your outfit.

Leaving the message, 'Call me back, I'm on my mobile.'
Get off it, it must be uncomfortable!

Talking on your mobile constantly while checking into a
hotel or a flight.

Be discreet, only do it in private.

Look mum – no hands! Use a hands-free car kit while driving.

Whenever ring tones might be intrusive, switch to vibrator.

If you're expecting a call and need to go into a meeting, leave your mobile with the receptionist.

Ask your receiver if they're on hands-free before you get too familiar.

Turn on alternative services and explore your options.

Switching your mobile to vibrator and driving with it in your lap.

Remembering to turn your mobile off before your ring tones interrupt anything from a spine-tingling aria to a lustful, unbridled and uncontrollable moment of passion.

Mastering the mobile phone conundrum: knowing how you are going to react when you receive a mobile call in the most embarassing place imaginable, and everyone is glaring at you for disturbing the peace. Will you drop everything and answer it? Will you ignore it and hope it will go away? Will you hide behind something and answer it in a whisper? Or will you run away in embarassment after causing a scene?

Answering your mobile during bidding at an auction and missing the fall of the hammer (and then having to offer the successful bidder more money to get your dream home).

Talking on your mobile while having a stress-relief massage.

Leaving your mobile on during the night.

Never being able to turn your mobile off, even when you're with your therapist.

Waiting at the airport baggage carousel and talking on your mobile. Still talking on your mobile while hailing a taxi. Still on your mobile on the way to your office, entering your office, walking to your secretary's desk – while you're still talking to her.

Calling from your mobile while standing next to a phone booth.

Tearing the house apart looking for your mobile.

Checking for messages before you're off the air-bridge and through the gate.

SAFE PHONE SEX

Leaving your mobile on during sex and worse, answering the mobile during sex and even worse, the caller's your other lover.

A news cameraman taking a call and missing a never-to-be-repeated moment in time.

Refusing to go somewhere because the location's out of range.

Answering your mobile when it's not yours that's ringing.

Taking calls in a church, synagogue or at a funeral.

Spending the entire evening on your mobile doing deals at your new flame's dinner party to meet their friends/family.

Having an epidural so you can continue mobile intercourse.

Sitting on the sofa with the mobile between you and your partner. The only things turned on are you and your mobile.

Having double call waiting – three calls at once!

(While these stories are true, we have not included any
names to protect the innocent.)

In the CBD around lunchtime, a business suit was deep in conversation
on their mobile (deal-crunching, saving the world?). A reporter
walked by, hoping for the inside story … 'Foccacia with sundried
tomatoes and bocconcini, no salt …'

A 12-year-old whipped out a mobile during class. This mobile phoney had forgotten to pack lunch and was calling mum for immediate delivery.

A rather shy guy, who hadn't even got to first base with his new girlfriend, finally plucked up the courage to lean over for a first kiss, and his trousers started to vibrate. Can you imagine how disappointed she was to find it was only his vibrating mobile ...

A cardiologist instructed a nurse to answer his ringing mobile during surgery. It was the previous night's date calling to thank him for a memorable evening. 'Ask her if she'll go out with me again,' he said to the nurse. The nurse replied, 'She said she'll think about it, it wasn't that memorable.' The surgeon said, 'She's only kidding!'

In a suburban shopping centre, a mother was pushing her toddlers in a stroller. What a scene. Not only was the mother walking and talking on the mobile, but her two littlies were also chewing the fat on their phones.

While out for spin one pleasant Saturday afternoon, a careless driver accidentally ran into the back of a four-wheel-drive. Speaking on a mobile, the driver of the four-wheel-drive was heard to say, 'I have to hang up now, I'm having an accident.'

At lunch, two recently divorced 40-something male executives were discussing their ex-wives – particularly how they were going to prevent them from getting the millions. Unknowingly, one of the men hit the dreaded redial key on his mobile phone, connecting with the ex-wife. She taped the lot and promptly delivered the tape to her lawyer.

Two colleagues of the opposite sex took a taxi to a meeting. During the taxi ride, they were entertained by the driver's pornographic tape playing softly in the background. Later that day, the woman drove her CEO to another meeting and answered her mobile on speaker phone. Her overly excited colleague from the taxi ride earlier bellowed with no introduction, 'Are you masturbating yet?'

A married couple were discussing what to buy a friend's newborn. The wife suggested a mobile. The husband, momentarily puzzled, asked, 'Isn't he too young for a mobile?'

During a visit to his sister's house, a mobile dependant excused himself to go to the toilet. A minute later, he came out of the toilet screaming with wet trousers and everything hanging out. His ringing mobile had dropped into the toilet and zapped him. Oouch!

After a boozy Friday lunch, a stockbroker returned to his office while talking on his mobile. As he entered his office, his desk phone rang. He answered the phone, saying, 'I'll be with you in a minute' and continued the mobile phone conversation with his mate – without putting his caller on hold. 'We're meeting at … at 5.30, all the boys will be there and we've got seven girls lined up.' After finishing this conversation, he went back to his desk phone, only to find that it was his wife on the other end.

An anaesthetist answered his mobile phone during a patient's knee operation. The patient had an epidural instead of a general anaesthetic, so he was awake throughout the procedure. When the anaesthetist finished his call, the patient borrowed his phone, called his office and proceeded to give a blow-by-blow description of what was happening, sound effects and all, commenting on how amazing it was that he could still run his business while in surgery.

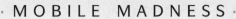

A woman was seated in a restaurant when her mobile phone rang. She took the phone out of her bag and answered the call, saying, 'I told you not to ring me on this number!' She put the phone away and then there was another call. She took another phone out of her bag and answered it, saying, 'That's better!'

An upwardly mobile banker flying first class offered a flight attendant his mobile phone number – all six of them! Pocket, car, boat, North America, Europe and GPS for when he's fishing or four-wheel-driving.

An eccentric allegedly hijacked a bus and demanded, 'Everyone throw your mobiles into the bag.' Pity he doesn't make restaurant calls.

A former eligible bachelor whisked his new bride away to Monte Carlo for a no-expense-spared honeymoon. On his return, he discovered that his mobile phone bill during the extravaganza had cost more than the honeymoon itself.

Don't wear a mobile on your belt, no matter how state-of-the-art it is.

If you don't want to raise the judge's eyebrows during cross-examination, avoid wearing your mobile on vibrator under your robes.

Don't use other people's mobiles without permission. However, borrowing a phoney's mobile on display is permitted – they're asking for it to be appreciated.

Don't let your mobile come between you and your partner.

Don't take calls in a restaurant unless World War III has broken out and you are vital to the peace process.

Don't gesticulate and wave your arms about while talking on your mobile, the receiver can hear you just as well if you keep still.

Don't bath with your partner and your mobile – you both may get more than you bargain for.

Don't use your mobile during flight unless you want to prematurely end it.

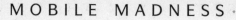

While you're in a meeting, it's not a good idea to leave your mobile on vibrator in your handbag.

Be careful when reaching for your mobile from your shoulder holster in shady cafes or neighbourhoods.

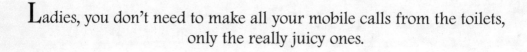

Ladies, you don't need to make all your mobile calls from the toilets, only the really juicy ones.

Definition of living dangerously: checking on your partner's fidelity by taking their mobile to find out who calls.

It makes me look successful.

It makes me look indispensable.

It impresses people.

It overcomes my inadequacies.

It makes me look important.

It makes me look sexy.

It makes me look exciting.

It makes me look popular.

NINETIES COWBOYS

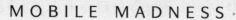

Women think it symbolises my penis (hard, black, busy, flashing, engaged, exciting).

Can't get ahead without it.

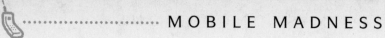

Confucius say, 'Person of great importance has no need for mobile' ...

... Have you ever seen Kerry or Rupert use one?